PLANT CLOSINGS

A Selected Bibliography

of Materials Published 1986 through 1990

Compiled by

Carla M. Weiss

1991

Martin P. Catherwood Library
New York State School of Industrial and Labor Relations
Cornell University
Ithaca, New York

Library of Congress Cataloging-in-Publication Data

Weiss, Carla M., 1951-
    Plant closings : a selected bibliography of
materials published 1986 through 1990 / compiled by
Carla M. Weiss.
         p.   cm.
    Includes index.
    ISBN 0-87546-801-2
    1. Plant shutdowns--United States--Bibliography.
2. Manpower policy--United States--Bibliography.
I. Martin P. Catherwood Library. II. Title.
Z7164.U56W46   1991
[HD5708.55.U6]
016.3386'042--dc20   91-8328

Copies of this bibliography can be ordered from

ILR Press
School of Industrial and Labor Relations
Cornell University
Ithaca, N.Y. 14853-3901

607/255-2264

Preface

There has been considerable material published in recent years on the subject of plant closings, their impact on communities, and the subsequent dislocation of workers. The Worker Adjustment and Retraining Notification Act of 1988, which requires that employers give advance notification of plant closings, has generated additional literature on the topic. Many of the publications in this bibliography focus on public policy issues, research findings or case studies. The sources include books, dissertations, government reports, working papers, and articles from scholarly and professional journals, general interest magazines and labor union periodicals or newspapers. The bibliography is intended to provide a comprehensive listing of publications in the collections of the Cornell University Library system, with emphasis on the Martin P. Catherwood Library. This volume contains items published from 1986 though 1990. A volume covering material published though 1985 was issued in 1988.

The bibliography is arranged alphabetically by author (usually a person, but in some instances the business or governmental organization which issued the publication). If no author is indicated, the item is listed under title. Each entry is numbered and is accompanied by subject headings, assigned from a pre-determined list of topics relating to the issue of plant closings. There are also subject headings for geographic areas and types of industries. Alphabetical indexes by subject heading and author appear at the end of the bibliography and refer to the number of the entry.

Many of the items listed in the bibliography were first identified by searching the online databases available through information retrieval services, such as DIALOG Information Service, Bibliographic Retrieval Service (BRS), and the Research Libraries Information Network (RLIN).

I would like to thank the following people:

Fran Benson for offering to have this publication distributed by the ILR Press; Helen Hamilton, Deanna Quvus, and Pat Rinchack for retrieving material included in the bibliography from all the libraries at Cornell; Steve Helmer for his technological advice and assistance; and finally Shirley Harper, Director of the Catherwood Library, for her encouragement and support.

Carla M. Weiss
Reference Librarian
Martin P. Catherwood Library

TABLE OF CONTENTS

1. Abbey, Michael H. "State Plant Closing Legislation: A Modern Justification for the Use of the Dormant Commerce Clause as a Bulwark of National Free Trade." <u>Virginia Law Review</u>, (May 1989): 845-894.

   Court or Board Decisions/Legislation - United States -States/ Worker Adjustment and Retraining Notification Act

2. Abrams, James L. "Plant Closings: New Requirements for Business." <u>Colorado Lawyer</u>, (Mar. 1989): 471-472.

   Legislation - United States/Worker Adjustment and Retraining Notification Act

3. Addison, John T. "The Controversy over Advance Notice Legislation in the United States." <u>British Journal of Industrial Relations</u>, (July 1989): 235-263.

   Advance Notice/Impact - Economic/Legislation - United States - States/Legislation - United States

4. Addison, John T. "Job Security in the United States: Law, Collective Bargaining, Policy, and Practice." <u>British Journal of Industrial Relations</u>, (Nov. 1986): 381-418.

   Court or Board Decisions/Collective Bargaining/Employment Security/Legislation - United States

5. Addison, John T.; Portugal, Pedro. "The Effect of Advance Notification of Plant Closings on Unemployment/Job Loss and Job Change: Comment." <u>Industrial and Labor Relations Review</u>, (Oct. 1987): 3-16,43-45,49.

   Advance Notice/Data Analysis/Unemployed

6. Addison, John T.; Portugal, Pedro. "Job Displacement, Relative Wage Changes, and Duration of Unemployment." <u>Journal of Labor Economics</u>, 7: 3 (July 1989): 281-302.

   Economic Models/Data Analysis/Impact - Earnings

7. "Advance Notice of Plant Closings." <u>Futurist</u>, 2 (Mar.-Apr. 1987): 49-50.

    Advance Notice/Assistance Programs

8. Album, Michael J. "'Of Taxes and Notices': Recent Developments under the Internal Revenue Code and WARN." <u>Employment Relations Today</u>, 17: 3 (Autumn 1990): 193-200.

    Advance Notice/Worker Adjustment and Retraining Notification Act

9. Ashton, Patrick J.; Iadicola, Peter. "Financial Impact of a Plant Closing on Displaced Blue-Collar and White-Collar Workers." <u>Labor Studies Journal</u>, 13: 1 (Spring 1988): 35-57.

    Case Studies/Geographic Location Study - United States Indiana/Impact - Earnings/White Collar Employees

10. Austin, Phyllis. "The Making of a One-Company Ghost Town." <u>Business and Society Review</u>, (Summer 1987): 59-64.

    Geographic Location Study - United States - Maine/Impact - Community - Case Studies/Industry - Paper

11. <u>Avoiding Plant Closings in New York State: An Integrated Approach: July 1986 Report</u>. Ithaca, N.Y.: New York State School of Industrial and Labor Relations, Division of Extension and Public Service, Cornell University, 1986. 54 p.

    Geographic Location Study - United States - New York/Labor-Management Relations/Preventive Measures

12. Badenfuller, Charles; Longley, Roger. "Predicting Plant Closures in European Industry." <u>Long Range Planning</u>, 21: 1 (1988): 90-96.

    Causes - Economic/Geographic Location Study - Europe/Industry - Chemical

13. Bahl, Roy. "Industrial Policy and the States: How Will They Pay?" <u>Journal of the American Planning Association</u>, 52: 3 (Summer 1986): 310-318.

    Economic Development Programs/Government Programs/Geographic Location Study - United States - States

14. Baker, Andrew M. "Plant Closings: Lessons from the Maine Experience." <u>Human Resource Management</u>, (Fall 1988): 315-328.

    Advance Notice/Geographic Location Study - United States - Maine/Legislation - United States - Maine

15. Barbee, George E. L. "Downsizing with Dignity: Easing the Pain of Employee Layoffs." <u>Business and Society Review</u>, (Spring 1987): 31-34.

    Assistance Programs/Human Resource Planning/Layoff

16. Barbee, George E. L. "Downsizing with Dignity: Trends in Employee Reduction Programs." <u>Price Waterhouse Review</u>, 3: 3 (1986): 6-15.

    Assistance Programs/Corporate Planning/Layoff

17. Barber, Floyd. <u>Bethlehem Steel Impact Study: Survey of Workers</u>. Albany, N.Y.: New York State Dept. of Labor, Division of Research and Statistics, 1988. 36 p.

    Impact - Case Studies/Geographic Location Study - United States - New York/Industry - Steel

18. Bartholomew, Susan. <u>Retraining Decisions of Older Displaced Workers</u>. Ph.D. Dissertation, University Of California, Los Angeles, 1987. 161 leaves.

    Older Workers - Case Studies/Retraining

19. Beaird, J. Ralph. "Relations of Employers with Workers' Representatives in the United States." <u>Georgia Journal of International and Comparative Law</u>, 16 (Spring 1986): 219-226.

    Collective Bargaining/Collective Bargaining - Duty to Bargain

20. Beckett, Joyce O. "Plant Closings: How Older Workers Are Affected." <u>Social Work</u>, (Jan.-Feb. 1988): 29-33.

    Impact - Economic/Impact - Psychological/Older Workers

21. Bee, Richard H.; Beronja, Terry Ann. "College Student Expectations: A Function of Their Socio-Economic Background." <u>College Student Journal</u>, 21: 2 (Summer 1987): 125-133.

    Geographic Location Study - United States - Ohio/Impact - Family/Impact - Higher Education

22. Benenson, Bob. "Members Hustle to Protect Defense Jobs Back Home." <u>Congressional Quarterly Weekly Report</u>, 48: 2 (Jan. 13, 1990): 87-90.

    Impact - Community/Industry - Defense

23. Bensman, David; Lynch, Roberta. <u>Rusted Dreams: Hard Times in a Steel Community</u>. New York: McGraw-Hill, 1987. 250 p.

    Geographic Location Study - United States - Illinois/Impact - Community/Impact - Economic/Industry - Steel

24. Berenbeim, Ronald. <u>Company Programs to Ease the Impact of Shutdowns</u>. (Conference Board report ; no. 878) New York: Conference Board, 1986. 57 p.

    Assistance Programs/Case Studies/Corporate Planning

25. Berry, Steve; Gottschalk, Peter; Wissoker, Doug. "An Error Components Model of the Impact of Plant Closing on Earnings." _Review of Economics & Statistics_, (Nov. 1988): 701-707.

    Economic Models/Impact - Earnings

26. Birch, David L. "Is Manufacturing Dead?" _Inc._, 9: 7 (June 1987): 35-36.

    Industry - Manufacturing

27. Blanpain, R. "Voluntary Plant Closings and Workforce Reductions: An International Perspective." _Georgia Journal of International and Comparative Law_, 16 (Spring 1986): 255-258.

    International Comparative Study/International Labour Organisation/Legislation/Organisation for Economoc Co-operation and Development

28. Blanquet, F. "Harmonization of Labor Law in the EEC." _Georgia Journal of International and Comparative Law_, 16 (Spring 1986): 267-269.

    Geographic Location Study - European Economic Community/ International Comparative Study/Legislation

29. Bradley, Keith. "Employee-Ownership and Economic Decline in Western Industrial Democracies." _Journal of Management Studies_, (Jan. 1986): 51-71.

    Employee Ownership

30. Brittain, Brian K.; Heshizer, Brian P. "Management Decision Bargaining: The Interplay of Law and Politics." _Labor Law Journal_, 38: 4 (Apr. 1987): 220-235.

    Collective Bargaining - Duty to Bargain/Court or Board Decisions

31. Browning, Martin. "Co-Operatives, Closures, or Wage Cuts: The Choices Facing Workers in an Ailing Firm." <u>Canadian Journal of Economics</u>, (Feb. 1987): 114-122.

    Concessions/Economic Models/Employee Ownership

32. Bruno, Robert A. "Remembering 'Black Monday': Steel Valley Revisited." <u>Workplace Democracy</u>, 60 (Spring 1988): 6-9.

    Geographic Location Study - United States - Ohio/Impact - Community - Case Studies/Industry - Steel

33. Burke, Ronald J. "Reemployment on a Poorer Job after a Plant Closing." <u>Psychological Reports</u>, (Apr. 1986): 559-570.

    Geographic Location Study - Canada/Impact - Earnings/Impact - Psychological/Reemployment

34. Buss, Terry F.; Vaughan, Roger J. <u>On the Rebound: Helping Workers Cope with Plant Closings</u>. Washington, D.C.: Council of State Policy and Planning Agencies, 1988. 99 p.

    Assistance Programs/Geographic Location Study - United States - Ohio/Government Programs/Impact - Community

35. Bussey, Jane; Sheets, Kenneth R.; Gest, Ted; Taylor, Ronald A.; Sandford, Gillian. "Political Punch-out over Plant Closings." <u>U.S. News & World Report</u>, 105: 3 (July 18, 1988): 8-9.

    Advance Notice/Legislation - United States

36. Byrne, Edmund F. "Building Community into Property." <u>Journal of Business Ethics</u>, 7 (Mar. 1988): 171-183.

    Impact - Community/Right of Property

37. Cagan, Steve. "Industrial Hostages." <u>Society</u>, 25: 5 (July-Aug. 1988): 82-85.

   Impact - Community/Impact - Employees/Unemployed

38. Caplan, Sorrell. "IBEW Strategy Helps to Avoid Plant Closings." <u>Work in America</u>, 13: 6 (June 1988): 3-5.

   Labor Unions/Labor-Management Relations/Preventive Measures

39. Carr, Steven D. "Managing the Business Risks of Plant Closings." <u>Business Horizons</u>, 33: 3 (May/June 1990): 72-74.

   Corporate Planning/Public Relations

40. Carroll, Charles T., Jr. "Plant Closings Nuances: Avoiding Last Minute Compliance Difficulties." <u>Labor Law Journal</u>, 39: 9 (Sept. 1988): 637-646.

   Advance Notice/Legislation - United States/Worker Adjustment and Retraining Notification Act

41. Castro, Felipe G.; Romero, Gloria J.; Cervantes, Richard C. "Long-Term Stress among Latino Women after a Plant Closure." <u>Sociology and Social Research</u>, 71: 2 (Jan. 1987): 85-88.

   Impact - Family/Impact - Psychological/Impact - Women/Industry - Canneries

42. Charpentier, Elaine. "Early Warnings in Chicago." <u>Labor Research Review</u>, 5: 2 (Fall 1986): 90-97.

   Geographic Location Study - United States - Illinois/Impact - Community/Preventive Measures

43. Christie, Innis. "Voluntary Plant Closings and Workforce Reductions in Canada." <u>Georgia Journal of International and Comparative Law</u>, 16 (Spring 1986): 249-254.

   Geographic Location Study - Canada/Layoff/Legislation - Canada

44. Clark, Gordon L. "Restructuring the U.S. Economy: The NLRB, the Saturn Project, and Economic Justice." <u>Economic Geography</u>, 62: 14 (Oct. 1986): 289-306.

   Court or Board Decisions/Industry - Automobile/Labor-Management Relations - Case Studies/National Labor Relations Board/Plant Relocation

45. "Closing Law's Key Provisions." <u>Nation's Business</u>, (Jan. 1989): 58-59.

   Legislation - United States/Worker Adjustment and Retraining Notification Act

46. <u>Closing Plants: Planning and Implementing Strategies</u>. Morristown, N.J.: Financial Executives Research Foundation, 1986. 104 p. By Coopers & Lybrand.

   Corporate Planning/Human Resource Planning

47. Cochrane, Brenda. "Union Maids No More: Long-term Impact of Loss of a Union Job on Women Workers." <u>Labor Studies Journal</u>, 13: 1 (Spring 1988): 19-34.

   Case Studies/Impact - Economic/Industry - Textile/Women in Labor Unions

48. Cochrane, Brenda. <u>Women and Plant Closures: What Is the Long-term Impact of the Loss of a Union Job?</u>. (Working paper series ; WPS 87-13) Columbus, Ohio: Business Research, College of Business, Ohio State University, 1987. 18 p.

   Impact - Women/Industry - Textile/Women in Labor Unions

49. Coil, James H., III. "Washington Scene." <u>Employment Relations Today</u>, (Summer 1989): 147-153.

   Advance Notice/Legislation - United States/Worker Adjustment and Retraining Notification Act

50. Collins, Denis. "Plant Closings: Establishing Legal Obligations." <u>Labor Law Journal</u>, 40 (Feb. 1989): 67-80.

   Advance Notice/Court or Board Decisions/Legislation - United States

51. Colosi, Marco L. "WARN: Hazardous to HR Health?" <u>Personnel</u>, (Apr. 1989): 59-67.

   Advance Notice/Human Resource Planning/Legislation - United States/Worker Adjustment and Retraining Notification Act

52. Committee for Economic Development. Research and Policy Committee. <u>Work and Change: Labor Market Adjustment Policies in a Competitive World</u>. New York, N.Y.: Committee for Economic Development, 1987. 76 p.

   Corporate Planning/Government Programs/Reemployment

53. Cooper, Matthew; Holmes, Allan. "The Disaster That Never Happened." <u>U.S. News & World Report</u>, 108: 8 (Feb. 26, 1990): 47.

   Worker Adjustment and Retraining Notification Act

54. Cooper, Syretha French. <u>The Ameliorative Effects of Social Support on Unemployment Related Stress</u>. Ph.D. Dissertation, Case Western Reserve University, 1988. 197 leaves.

   Assistance Programs/Impact - Physiological/Impact - Psychological

55. <u>Coping with Corporate Change: Labor Law Issues Affecting Plant Closings, Joint Ventures, Acquisitions and Other Corporate Restructuring: Course Materials</u>. Washington, D.C.: Bureau of National Affairs, 1989.

    Collective Bargaining/Court or Board Decisions/ Discrimination/ Legislation - United States

56. Cornfield, Daniel B. "Plant Shutdowns and Union Decline: The United Furniture Workers of America, 1963-1981." <u>Work and Occupations</u>, (Aug. 1987): 434-451.

    Industry - Furniture Making/Labor Unions

57. Cotton, John L.; Majchrzak, Ann. "Psychological Predictors of Geographical Relocation: Case Study of a Plant Shutdown." <u>Journal of Business & Psychology</u>, 4: 3 (Spring 1990): 375-384.

    Employee Relocation - Case Studies/Impact - Psychological

58. Craypo, Charles. "Industrial Restructuring Following Plant Closings and Phasedowns." <u>Labor Law Journal</u>, 39: 8 (Aug. 1988): 557-562.

    Geographic Location Study - United States - Indiana/Industry

59. Cronin, Frank; Lacey, Inese. "WARNA Warnings: The New Federal Plant Closing Law." <u>The Practical Lawyer</u>, (Jan. 1989): 81-90.

    Legislation - United States/Worker Adjustment and Retraining Notification Act

60. Curtain, Richard. "After Retrenchment: Labour Market Experiences of Women and Men." <u>Australian Journal of Social Issues</u>, 22: 4 (Feb. 1987): 357-375.

    Geographic Location Study - Australia/Impact - Women - Case Studies/Reemployment

61. Daniels, Gene. "American Cranes Fly South." <u>Labor Law Journal</u>, 39: 8 (Aug. 1988): 534-538.

    Case Studies/Plant Relocation

62. De Bernardo, Mark A. "Handling the Ultimate Personnel Disaster: Business Closings and Mass Layoffs." <u>Security</u>, (Mar. 1989): 27-30.

    Assistance Programs/Corporate Planning

63. DeBow, Yvette. "G.E.: Easing the Pain of Layoffs." <u>Management Review</u>, (Sept. 1987): 15-18.

    Assistance Programs/Geographic Location Study - United States - Maryland/Industry - Electrical/Reemployment Planning - Case Studies

64. Deery, Stephen; Griffin, Gerard; Brown, Michelle; Dowling, Peter. "The Labour Market Experience of Redundant Workers: A Study of a Plant Closure." <u>Australian Bulletin of Labour</u>, 12: 3 (June 1986): 173-194.

    Geographic Location Study - Australia/Impact - Earnings/ Industry - Brewing/Reemployment - Case Studies/Unemployed

65. Deily, Mary E. "Investment Activity and the Exit Decision." <u>Review of Economics and Statistics</u>, 70: 4 (Nov. 1988): 595-602.

    Economic Models/Investments

66. <u>Deindustrialization and Plant Closure</u>. Lexington, Mass.: D.C. Heath, 1987. 348 p. Edited by Paul D. Staudohar and Holly E. Brown.

    Deindustrialization/Legislation - United States

67. Deindustrialization and Regional Economic Transformation: The Experience of the United States. Boston: Unwin Hyman, 1989. 319 p. Edited by Lloyd Rodwin and Hidehiko Sazanami.

    Deindustrialization/Regional Planning

68. Desolre, Guy. "Voluntary Plant Closings and Workforce Reductions in Belgium." Georgia Journal of International and Comparative Law, 16: (Spring 1986): 241-247.

    Geographic Location Study - Belgium/Layoff/Legislation - Belgium

69. Devens, Richard M., Jr. "Displaced Workers: One Year Later." Monthly Labor Review, 109: 7 (July 1986): 40-43.

    Longitudinal Study/Reemployment/Unemployed

70. Dislocated Workers: Expenditures under Title III of the Job Training Parternship Act: Fact Sheet for the Chairman, Committee on Education and Labor, House of Representatives. Washington, D.C.: General Accounting Office, 1990. 24 p.

    Data Analysis/Government Programs/Impact - Economic/Job Training Partnership Act

71. Doherty, Barbara. The Struggle to Save Morse Cutting Tool: A Successful Community Campaign. North Dartmouth, Mass.: Arnold M. Dubin Labor Education Center, Southeastern Massachusetts University, [1985 or 1986]. 34 p.

    Geographic Location Study - United States - Massachusetts/ Impact/Industry - Manufacturing - Case Studies/Labor Unions

72. Donahoe, Myrna Cherkoss. Workers' Response to Plant Closures: The Cases of Steel and Auto in Southeast Los Angeles, 1935-1986. Ph.D. Dissertation, University of California, Irvine, 1987. 380 leaves.

    Geographic Location Study - United States - California/ Industry - Automobile/Industry - Steel/Labor Unions

73. Dougherty, Jim; Stout, Mike. "Reindustrialization from the Bottom Up." <u>Social Policy</u>, (Winter 1988): 50-52.

    Deindustrialization/Economic Development Programs/Geographic Location Study - United States - Pennsylvania/Impact - Community/Industry - Steel

74. Douglas, James A. "State and Local Plant Closing Laws: The Case against Preemption." <u>Gonzaga Law Review</u>, 21: 3 (Oct. 1986): 603-674.

    Advance Notice/Collective Bargaining - Duty to Bargain/Court or Board Decisions/Legislation - United States - States/ National Labor Relations Act/Severance Pay

75. Drennan, Jan. "Responding to Industrial Plant Closings and the Unemployed." <u>Social Work</u>, (Jan.-Feb. 1988): 50-52.

    Geographic Location Study - United States - Illinois/Impact - Psychological/Labor Unions/Unemployed - Case Studies

76. Dresser, Karyn Lynn. <u>The Construction of Unemployment as a Social Problem: Powerlessness, Stigmitization and the Unemployed</u>. Ph.D. Dissertation, University of California, Santa Cruz, 1988. 317 leaves.

    Impact - Psychological/Impact - Social/Industry - Automobile - Case Studies/Unemployed

77. Dunne, Timothy; Roberts, Mark J.; Samuelson, Larry. "Plant Turnover and Gross Employment Flows in the U.S. Manufacturing Sector." <u>Journal of Labor Economics</u>, 7: 1 (Jan. 1989): 48-71.

    Data Analysis/Economic Models/Job Creation/Unemployed

78. <u>Economic Adjustment and Worker Dislocation in a Competitive Society: A Report of the Secretary of Labor's Task Force on Economic Adjustment and Worker Dislocation</u>. Washington, D.C.: The Task Force, 1986. 150 p.

    Assistance Programs/Government Programs

79. Edin, Per-Anders. <u>Individual Consequences of Plant Closures</u>.
    (Studia oeconomica Upsaliensia ; 15) Uppsala: Uppsala
    University, 1989. 99 p.

    Data Analysis/Geographic Location Study - Sweden/Impact -
    Earnings/Impact - Psychological/Reemployment/Unemployed

80. Ehrenberg, Ronald G. "Workers' Rights: Rethinking Protective
    Labor Legislation." <u>Research in Labor Economics</u>, 8B (1986):
    285-317.

    Advance Notice/Impact - Employees/Legislation - United States

81. Ehrenberg, Ronald G.; Jakubson, George H. <u>Advance Notice
    Provisions in Plant Closing Legislation: Do They Matter?</u>.
    (NBER working paper ; no. 2611) Cambridge, Mass.: National
    Bureau of Economic Research, 1988. 20 p.

    Advance Notice/Legislation - United States

82. Ehrenberg, Ronald G.; Jakubson, George H. <u>Advance Notice
    Provisions in Plant Closing Legislation</u>. Kalamazoo, Mich.:
    W.E. Upjohn Institute for Employment Research, 1988. 101 p.

    Advance Notice/Data Analysis/Legislation - United States/
    Unemployed

83. Ehrenberg, Ronald G.; Jakubson, George H. "Advance Notification
    of Plant Closing: Does It Matter?" <u>Industrial Relations</u>, 28:
    1 (Winter 1989): 60-71.

    Advance Notice/Impact/Unemployed

84. Ehrenberg, Ronald G.; Jakubson, George H. "Why WARN?: Plant
    Closing Legislation." <u>Regulation</u>, 13: 2 (Summer 1990): 39-46.

    Advance Notice/Legislation - United States/Worker Adjustment
    and Retraining Notification Act

85. Ekstrom, Brenda L.; Leistritz, F. Larry. <u>Plant Closure and</u>
    <u>Community Decline: An Annotated Bibliography</u>. Monticello,
    Ill.: Vance Bibliographies, 1986. 47 p.

    Bibliography/Impact - Community

86. Elston, Wille Edward. <u>A Followup Case Study of the Results of</u>
    <u>Retraining Displaced Workers: Four Years Later</u>. Ed.D.
    Dissertation, University of California, Los Angeles, 1988.
    176 leaves.

    Assistance Programs/Retraining - Case Studies

87. <u>Employee Buyout Handbook</u>. Revised edition. Arlington, Va.:
    National Center for Employee Ownership, 1986. 54 p. By
    Michael Kieschnik et al.

    Employee Ownership/Handbooks, Manuals, etc.

88. Fedrau, Ruth H.; Balfe, Kevin P. <u>Cooperative Labor-management</u>
    <u>Worker Adjustment Programs</u>. (BLMR ; 133) Washington, D.C.:
    U.S. Dept of Labor, Bureau of Labor-Management Relations and
    Cooperative Programs, 1989. 64 p.

    Assistance Programs - Case Studies/Cooperation/Labor-
    Management Relations

89. Fedrau, Ruth H.; Balfe, Kevin P. "Cooperative Labor-Management
    Worker Adjustment Programs." <u>Labor Law Journal</u>, 40: 3 (March
    1989): 138-149.

    Assistance Programs/Labor Unions/Labor-Management Relations

90. Feldman, Diane. "Helping Displaced Workers: The UAW-GM Human
    Resource Center." <u>Personnel</u>, (Mar. 1988): 34-36.

    Assistance Programs - Case Studies/Geographic Location Study
    - United States - Ohio/Industry - Automobile/Labor-Management
    Relations

91. Feldman, Diane. "Hope for Displaced Workers when a Plant
    Closes." Management Review, (Apr. 1988): 16-18.

    Assistance Programs/Geographic Location Study - United States
    - Ohio/Industry - Automobile/Reemployment Planning - Case
    Studies

92. Final Report of the Mature Industries Research Project on
    Partial Plant Closings. Boston: Commonwealth of
    Massachusetts, Division of Employment Security, 1986. 86
    leaves.

    Data Analysis/Geographic Location Study - United States -
    Massachusetts/Government Programs/Legislation - United States
    - Massachusetts

93. Fisher, Caricia. Back to Work: The States and Dislocated
    Workers. Washington, D.C.: National Alliance of Business,
    1988. 67 p.

    Government Programs/Job Training Partnership Act/Legislation
    - United States - States/Retraining

94. Flowers, Linda. Throwed Away: Failures of Progress in Eastern
    North Carolina. Knoxville: University of Tennessee Press,
    1990. 241 p.

    Geographic Location Study - United States - North Carolina/
    Impact - Social

95. Flynn, Patricia M. Evolving Responsibilities in Work Force
    Development: Incorporating the Dynamics of Change. Atlanta:
    American Pscyhological Association, 1988. 12 p. Paper
    presented at the Annual Meeting of the American Psychological
    Association (96th, Atlanta, GA, August 12-16, 1988).

    Human Resource Planning/Retraining/Skills

96. Franzem, Joseph J. "Easing the Pain." Personnel Administrator,
    (Feb. 1987): 48-55.

    Assistance Programs - Case Studies/Industry - Brewing

97. Fraze, James. "Displaced Workers: Okies of the '80s." Personnel Administrator, (Jan. 1988): 42-51.

    Advance Notice/Legislation - United States/Retraining

98. Frey, Donald N. "The Social Contract Is Threatened." Chief Executive, (May/June 1989): 10,14.

    Acquisitions and Mergers/Corporate Power

99. Friedman, Robert E. "Entrepreneurial Renewal in the Industrial City." Annals of the American Academy of Political and Social Science, 488 (Nov. 1986): 35-46.

    Job Creation/Investments/Reemployment

100. Fuechtmann, Thomas G. Steeples and Stacks: Religion and Steel Crisis in Youngstown. New York: Cambridge University Press, 1989. 308 p.

    Geographic Location Study - United States - Ohio/Impact - Community - Case Studies/Industry - Steel

101. Gallo, Judith. "An Analysis of Plant Closing Law: How to Protect Workers from the Effects of Cessation in Business while Preserving Employer Rights." John Marshall Law Review, 21: 3 (Spring 1988): 565-591.

    Advance Notice/Assistance Programs/Concessions/Court or Board Decisions/Legislation - United States/Legislation - United States - States

102. Galvin, Martin Jay; Lied, Michael Robert. "Severance Pay: A Liability in Waiting?" Personnel Journal, 65 (June 1986): 126-132.

    Court or Board Decisions/Severance Pay

103. "General Discussion: Roundtable on Comparative Labor
     Relations Law: the Law and Measures Affecting Workers in the
     Context of Voluntary Plant Closings and Workforce
     Reductions, Brussels, Belgium, July 11, 1985." <u>Georgia
     Journal of International and Comparative Law</u>, 16 (Spring
     1986): 271-284.

     International Comparative Study/Labor Unions/Layoff

104. Gerhart, Paul F. <u>Saving Plants and Jobs: Union-Management
     Negotiations in the Context of Threatened Plant Closing</u>.
     Kalamazoo, Mich.: W.E. Upjohn Institute for Employment
     Research, 1987. 109 p.

     Case Studies/Causes/Collective Bargaining/Labor-Management
     Relations

105. Gibbons, Robert. <u>Layoffs and Lemons</u>. (Working paper ; no.
     249) Princeton, N.J.: Industrial Relations Section,
     Princeton University, 1989. 41 p.

     Impact - Earnings/Layoff/Unemployed

106. Gibson, W. David; Hibbs, Mark; Pitman, Frank. "A Labor Union
     Wields 'PR' Weapons." <u>Chemical Week</u>, (Jan. 22, 1986): 57.

     Industry - Audio-visual Supplies/Labor Unions/Public
     Relations

107. Giloth, Robert; Rosenblum, Susan. "How to Fight Plant
     Closings." <u>Social Policy</u>, (Winter 1987): 20-26.

     Advance Notice - Case Studies/Geographic Location Study -
     United States - Illinois/Preventive Measures

108. Gorney, Carole. "How to Plan Ahead for Mass Layoffs." <u>Public
     Relations Journal</u>, (June 1986): 31-32, 35.

     Assistance Programs/Planning Programs/Public Relations

109. Gould, William B., IV. "Job Security in the United States: Some Reflections on Unfair Dismissal and Plant Closure Legislation from a Comparative Perspective." <u>Nebraska Law Review</u>, 67 (Winter-Spring 1988): 28-55.

     Employment Security/International Comparative Study/Layoff/ Legislation/Legislation - United States/Legislation - United States - States

110. Grayson, J. Paul. <u>Plant Closures and De-skilling: Three Case Studies: An Analysis of Skills, Wages, and Re-training of Former Employees of SKF Canada Ltd., Scarborough, CGE Scarborough, and Black and Decker, Barrie</u>. (Discussion paper) Ottawa: Science Council of Canada, 1986. 30 p.

     Case Studies/Geographic Location Study - Canada/ Reemployment/ Retraining

111. Grayson, J. Paul. "Plant Closures and Political Despair." <u>Canadian Review of Sociology and Anthropology</u>, 23: 3 (Aug. 1986): 331-349.

     Geographic Location Study - Canada - Ontario/Impact - Psychological/Impact - Social/Unemployed - Case Studies

112. Guskind, Robert. "Picking Up the Pieces." <u>Planning</u>, 56: 6 (June 1990): 12-16.

     Impact - Community/Industry - Defense

113. Hamermesh, Daniel S. <u>Labor Demand and the Structure of Adjustment Costs</u>. (NBER working paper series ; no. 2572) Cambridge, Mass.: National Bureau of Economic Research, 1988. 27 p.

     Economic Models/Productivity

114. Hamermesh, Daniel S. <u>Plant Closings, Labor Demand and the Value of the Firm</u>. (NBER working paper ; no. 1839) Cambridge, Mass.: National Bureau of Economic Research, 1986. 25 p.

Concessions/Economic Models

115. Hamermesh, Daniel S. "Plant Closings and the Value of the Firm." <u>Review of Economics & Statistics (Netherlands)</u>, (Nov. 1988): 580-586.

Concessions/Data Analysis/Economic Models

116. Hamermesh, Daniel S. <u>What Do We Know about Worker Displacement in the U.S.?</u>. (NBER working paper series ; no. 2402) Cambridge, Mass.: National Bureau of Economic Research, 1987. 12 p.

Impact - Earnings/Unemployed

117. Hamermesh, Daniel S. "What Do We Know About Worker Displacement in the U.S.?" <u>Industrial Relations</u>, (Winter 1989): 51-59.

Concessions/Impact - Employees/Unemployed

118. Hamilton, V. Lee; Broman, Clifford L.; Hoffman, William S.; Renner, Deborah S. "Hard Times and Vulnerable People: Initial Effects of Plant Closing on Autoworkers' Mental Health." <u>Journal of Health and Social Behavior</u>, 31 (June 1990): 123-140.

Impact - Psychological - Case Studies/Industry - Automobile/ Unemployed

119. Hampton, William J. "Reality Has Hit General Motors -- Hard." <u>Business Week</u>, (Nov. 24, 1986): 37.

Industry - Automobile - Case Studies/Labor-Management Relations

120. Hansen, Gary B. "American Labor and International Trade: Adjustment Strategies to Assist Workers Displaced in Plant Closings and Permanent Layoffs." Economia & Lavoro, 21: 1 (Jan.-Mar. 1987): 115-122.

Assistance Programs/Government Programs/Unemployed

121. Hansen, Gary B. "Creating a Future for Workers Displaced by Foreign Competition." Business Forum, (Winter 1988): 16-21.

Collective Bargaining - Contract Language/Foreign Competition/Foreign Trade Policy/Unemployed

122. Hansen, Gary B. "A Follow-Up Survey of Workers Displaced by the Ford San Jose Assembly Plant Closure." Industrial Relations Research Association. Proceedings of the Fortieth Meeting, (Dec. 28-30, 1987): 125-134.

Assistance Programs/Geographic Location Study - United States - California/Industry - Automobile/Labor-Management Relations

123. Hansen, Gary B. "Layoffs, Plant Closings, and Worker Displacement in America: Serious Problems That Need a National Solution." Journal of Social Issues, 44: 4 (1988): 153-171.

Causes - Economic/Government Programs/Legislation - United States

124. Hansen, Gary B. "Services to Workers Facing Plant Shutdowns: California and Canada." International Journal of Manpower, 7: 1 (1986): 35-52.

Assistance Programs - Case Studies/Geographic Location Study - Canada/Geographic Location Study - United States - California/Reemployment/Retraining

125. Hardy, Cynthia. "Effective Retrenchment: Human Resource
     Implications." <u>Journal of General Management</u>, 12: 3 (Spring
     1987): 76-92.

     Geographic Location Study - Canada/Geographic Location Study
     - Great Britain/Human Resource Planning/International
     Comparative Study

126. Harris, Michael M.; Heller, Tamar; Braddock, David. "Sex
     Differences in Psychological Well-Being During a Facility
     Closure." <u>Journal of Management</u>, (Sept. 1988): 391-402.

     Data Analysis/Impact - Psychological - Case Studies/Impact -
     Women

127. Harris, Stanley G.; Sutton, Robert I. "Functions of Parting
     Ceremonies in Dying Organizations." <u>Academy of Management
     Journal</u>, (Mar. 1986): 5-30.

     Corporate Planning/Impact - Psychological/Organizational
     Behavior

128. Harte, G. F.; Owen, D. L. "Fighting De-industrialisation: The
     Role of Local Government Social Audits." <u>Accounting,
     Organizations and Society</u>, 12: 2 (Apr. 1987): 123-141.

     Corporate Planning/Deindustrialization/Geographic Location
     Study - Great Britain/Impact - Economic/Impact - Social

129. Hedlund, Jeffrey D. "An Economic Case for Mandatory Bargaining
     over Partial Termination and Plant Relocation Decisions."
     <u>Yale Law Journal</u>, (Apr. 1986): 949-968.

     Collective Bargaining - Duty to Bargain/Court or Board
     Decisions/Plant Relocation

130. Herbert, Garry. "Company Closures: Performing the Last Rites."
     <u>Personnel Management</u>, (July 1986): 29-33.

     Assistance Programs/Corporate Planning/Geographic Location
     Study - Great Britain

131. Hill, Richard Child; Negrey, Cynthia. "Deindustrialization in the Great Lakes." *Urban Affairs Quarterly*, 22: 4 (June 1987): 580-597.

Data Analysis/Deindustrialization/Geographic Location Study - United States - Midwestern States

132. Hillman, Arye L.; Katz, Eliakim; Rosenberg, Jacob. "Workers as Insurance: Anticipated Government Assistance and Factor Demand." *Oxford Economic Papers*, 39: 4 (Dec. 1987): 813-820.

Economic Models/Government Programs

133. Hoerr, John P. *And the Wolf Finally Came: The Decline of the American Steel Industry*. (Pittsburgh series in social and labor history) Pittsburgh: University of Pittsburgh Press, 1988. 690 p.

Collective Bargaining/Geographic Location Study - United States - Pennsylvania/Geographic Location Study - United States - West Virginia/Industry - Steel/Labor Unions

134. Hoffman, Ellen. "Refitting Workers." *National Journal*, 18 (Dec. 20, 1986): 3072-3075.

Government Programs/Legislation - United States/ Reemployment/Retraining

135. Hofstetter, Karl A.; Klubeck, Richard A. "Accommodating Labor and Community Interests in Mass Dismissals: A Transnational Approach." *Industrial Relations Law Journal*, 9: 3 (1987): 451-496.

Collective Bargaining - Duty to Bargain/Foreign Competition/ International Comparative Study/Legislation/Multinational Corporations

136. Hogan, Bill. "Plant Closings - A Hot Potato." *D & B Reports*, 36: 4 (July-Aug. 1988): 50-51.

Acquisitions and Mergers/Advance Notice/Legislation - United States

137. Hornack, Joseph S.; Lynd, Staughton; Clavel, Pierre; Hanratty, Patricia. "The Steel Valley Authority." <u>New York University Review of Law & Social Change</u>, 15: 1 (Winter 1987): 113-146.

Economic Development Programs/Geographic Location Study - United States - Pennsylvania/Industry - Steel/Preventive Measures

138. Horvath, Francis W. "The Pulse of Economic Change: Displaced Workers of 1981-85." <u>Monthly Labor Review</u>, 110: 6 (June 1987): 3-12.

Data Analysis/Reemployment/Unemployed

139. Hosmer, LaRue Tone. "Ethical Analysis and Human Resource Management." <u>Human Resource Management</u>, 26: 3 (Fall 1987): 313-330.

Ethics/Human Resource Planning

140. "How Americans Get the Sack." <u>The Economist</u>, 304 (July 18-24, 1987): 27-28.

Advance Notice/Unemployed

141. Howell, Robert E.; Bentley, Marion T. <u>Assessing, Managing, and Mitigating the Impacts of Economic Decline: A Community Perspective</u>. (WREP ; 91) Corvallis, Ore.: Western Rural Development Center, Oregon State University, 1986. 12 p.

Assistance Programs/Impact - Community/Impact - Family

142. Howland, Marie. <u>Plant Closings and Worker Displacement: The Regional Issues</u>. Kalamazoo, Mich.: W.E. Upjohn Institute for Employment Research, 1988. 172 p.

Causes/Deindustrialization/Government Programs/Impact - Economic/Unemployed

143. Howland, Marie. "Plant Closures and Local Economic Conditions." <u>Regional Studies</u>, 22: 3 (June 1988): 193-207.

    Causes/Causes - Imports/Economic Models/Foreign Competition/ Labor Unions

144. Howland, Marie. "Plant Closures and Worker Displacement." <u>Journal of Planning Literature</u>, 3: 1 (Winter 1988): 1-21.

    Causes/Impact - Employees/Planning Programs

145. Howland, Marie; Peterson, George E. <u>Labor Market Conditions and the Reemployment of Displaced Workers</u>. (Urban studies working paper ; no. 6) Washington, D.C.: Urban Institute, 1986. 29 leaves.

    Impact - Employees/Reemployment

146. Howland, Marie; Peterson, George E. "Labor Market Conditions and the Reemployment of Displaced Workers." <u>Industrial and Labor Relations Review</u>, (Oct. 1988): 109-122.

    Data Analysis/Impact - Earnings/Reemployment/White Collar Employees

147. Howland, Marie; Peterson, George E. "The Response of City Economies to National Business Cycles." <u>Journal of Urban Economics</u>, 23: 1 (Jan. 1988): 71-85.

    Causes - Economic/Data Analysis/Urban Economics

148. Hurst, Joe B.; Shepard, John W. "The Dynamics of Plant Closings: An Extended Emotional Roller Coaster Ride." <u>Journal of Counseling and Development</u>, 64: 6 (Feb. 1986): 401-405.

    Assistance Programs/Impact - Psychological - Case Studies

149. "An Introduction to Plant Closing Law." <u>Res Gestae</u>, (Sept. 1988): 144-145.

  Legislation - United States/Worker Adjustment and Retraining Notification Act

150. Jacobs, Antoine. "Voluntary Plant Closings and Workforce Reductions in the Netherlands." <u>Georgia Journal of International and Comparative Law</u>, 16: 2 (Spring 1986): 235-239.

  Geographic Location Study - Netherlands/Labor Unions/ Legislation - Netherlands

151. Jannotta, Joseph. "Stroh's Outplacement Success." <u>Management Review</u>, (Jan. 1987): 52-53.

  Assistance Programs - Case Studies/Geographic Location Study - United States - Michigan/Industry - Brewing

152. Jenish, D'Arcy. "Slippery Roads for GM." <u>Maclean's</u>, 1 (Feb. 23, 1987): 36-38.

  Foreign Competition/Geographic Location Study - Canada/ Geographic Location Study - United States/Industry - Automobile/Productivity

153. Jones, Clifford L. "Plant Closings: The Business View." <u>Duquesne Law Review</u>, 26 (Winter 1988): 419-423.

  Causes - Economic/Corporate Planning/Legislation - United States

154. Juravich, Tom; Gall, Gilbert J. <u>Pennsylvania Trade Unions and Worker Dislocation: Experiences and Attitudes: A Research Report to the Pennsylvania AFL-CIO</u>. Pennsylvania: Pennsylvania AFL-CIO, 1989. 12 p.

  Assistance Programs/Geographic Location Study - United States - Pennsylvania/Labor Unions

155. Kassalow, Everett M. "Employee Training and Development: A Joint Union-Management Response to Structural and Technological Change." <u>Industrial Relations Research Association. Proceedings of the Fortieth Annual Meeting</u>, (Dec. 28-30, 1987): 107-117.

     Assistance Programs/Labor Unions/Labor-Management Relations/Retraining

156. Keeley, Michael. "Individual Rights and Organizational Theory." <u>Employee Responsibilities and Rights Journal</u>, 1: 1 (Mar. 1988): 25-38.

     Concessions/Corporate Power/Employee Rights

157. Kerson, Roger. <u>State and Local Initiatives on Development Subsidies and Plant Closings</u>. Chicago: Federation for Industrial Retention and Renewal, 1989. 107 p.

     Economic Development Programs/Legislation - United States - States

158. Kinicki, Angelo; Bracker, Jeffrey; Kreitner, Robert; Lockwood, Chris; Lemak, David. "Socially Responsible Plant Closings." <u>Personnel Administrator</u>, (June 1987): 116-128.

     Corporate Planning/Impact - Employees/Legislation - United States

159. Kline, Paula. <u>A Developmental Exploration</u>. Ed.D. Dissertation, Harvard University, 1986. 207 leaves.

     Impact - Psychological/Unemployed

60. Kovach, Kenneth A.; Millspaugh, Peter E. "Plant Closings: Is the American Industrial Relations System Failing?" <u>Business Horizons</u>, (Mar./Apr. 1987): 44-49.

     Collective Bargaining/Court or Board Decisions/Legislation - United States/National Labor Relations Board

161. Krajci, Thomas J. "Outplacement En Masse: A Marketing Approach." _Personnel Administrator_, 32: 5 (May 1987): 90-94.

   Assistance Programs/Reemployment Planning - Case Studies

162. Kriegler, Roy; Sloan, Judy. _The Effects of Redundancy: The Closure of the Sterling Clothing Company Plant, Geelong._ (Working paper series ; no. 86) Bedford Park, S. Aust: National Institute of Labour Studies, Flinders University of South Australia, 1986. 29 p.

   Geographic Location Study - Australia/Impact - Employees/ Industry - Clothing - Case Studies/Unemployed

163. Kubasek, Nancy. "The Inevitable Conflict between Individualism and Plant Closing Legislation." _Legal Studies Forum_, 12: 2 (1988): 141-173.

   Impact - Economic/Impact - Social/Legislation - United States

164. Kubasek, Nancy. "Reframing the Argument for National Plant-closing Legislation." _Mid-American Journal of Business_, 2 (Mar. 1987): 15-20.

   Employee Rights/Legislation - United States/Unemployed

165. Kubasek, Nancy. "State Plant Closing Legislation and Preemption by ERISA." _Stetson Law Review_, 17: 2 (Spring 1988): 319-342.

   Employee Benefits/Legislation - United States - States/ Legislation - United States - Maine/Severance Pay

166. Kuhn, Dennis R.; Zech, Charles E. "Plant Closings and Public Policy: Achieving an Optimal Level of Plant Closings." _Law and Policy_, 10: 1 (Jan. 1988): 63-84.

   Court or Board Decisions/Impact - Community/Impact - Social/ Legislation - United States

167. <u>Labor Law and Business Change: Theoretical and Transactional Perspectives</u>. New York: Quorum Books, 1988. 353 p. Edited by Samuel Estreicher and Daniel G. Collins.

Labor Unions/Labor-Management Relations/Legislation - United States

168. LaRusso, Anthony C. "Shutting It Down: A Test for Management." <u>Business Horizons</u>, (July-Aug. 1989): 59-62.

Corporate Planning

169. Lauria, Mickey. "Toward a Specification of the Local State: State Intervention Strategies in Response to a Manufacturing Plant Closure." <u>Antipode</u>, 18: 1 (Apr. 1986): 39-63.

Economic Development Programs/Geographic Location Study - United States - Iowa/Impact - Community/Labor-Management Relations

170. "Layoffs: Pro and Con in WARN and Its Enforcement." <u>Work in America</u>, 14: 3 (Mar. 1989): 6-7.

Advance Notice/Worker Adjustment and Retraining Notification Act

171. Lazes, Peter. "Participative Consulting." <u>ILR Report</u>, (Fall 1988): 24-27.

Labor-Management Relations - Case Studies/Preventive Measures

172. Leadbeater, Charles. "Steeled for Closure Fight." <u>Management Today</u>, (July 1990): 25.

Geographic Location Study - Scotland/Industry - Steel/ Political Aspects

173. Leana, Carrie R.; Feldman, Daniel C. "Layoffs: How Employees and Companies Cope." Personnel Journal, 67: 9 (Sept. 1988): 31-34.

   Human Resource Planning/Impact - Psychological/Layoff

174. Legislative History of S. 2527, 100th Congress, Worker Adjustment and Retraining Notification Act, Public Law 100-379. Washington, D.C.: U.S. G.P.O., 1990. 847 p. Prepared for the Subcommittee on Labor-Management Relations of the Committee on Education and Labor.

   Legislation - United States/Worker Adjustment and Retraining Notification Act

175. Leki, Pete. "A Powerful Weapon against TNC's." Labor Today, 27: 1 (Spring 1988): 10-11.

   Labor Unions/Legislation/Multinational Corporations

176. Leroy, Greg; Swinney, Dan; Charpentier, Elaine. Early Warning Manual against Plant Closings. (Working papers ; no. 2) Chicago: Midwest Center for Labor Research, 1986. 71 p.

   Handbooks, Manuals, etc./Labor Unions/Preventive Measures

177. Lewis, John. "The Town That Puts Industry First." Business (UK), (Feb. 1988): 82-84.

   Geographic Location Study - Great Britain/Government Programs/Reemployment

178. Logue John ; Quilligan, James P.. ; Weissman, Barbara J. Buyout: Employee Ownership as an Alternative to Plant Shutdowns: the Ohio Experience. Kent, Ohio: Kent Popular Press, 1986. 98 p. Foreword by William F. Whyte.

   Employee Ownership - Case Studies/Geographic Location Study - United States - Ohio

179. Love, Colin. <u>Conflicts over Closure: the Laurence Scott Affair</u>. Aldershot, Hants, England: Avebury, 1988. 120 p.

    Acquisitions and Mergers - Case Studies/Geographic Location Study - Great Britain/Industry - Electrical/Labor Unions

180. Love, Douglas O.; Torrence, William D. "The Value of Advance Notice of Worker Displacement." <u>Southern Economic Journal</u>, (Jan. 1989): 626-643.

    Advance Notice/Data Analysis/Impact - Earnings/Layoff/ Unemployed

181. Lovell, Malcolm R. "The Task Force on Economic Adjustment and Worker Dislocation." <u>Industrial Relations Research Association. Proceedings of the Fortieth Annual Meeting</u>, (Dec. 28-30, 1987): 100-106.

    Advance Notice/Legislation - United States/Reemployment

182. Luce, Roger A. "Case IH/University of Wisconsin-Stout Cooperative Manufacturing Technology Project." <u>Economic Development Review</u>, (Winter 1988): 17-19.

    Cooperation/Economic Development Programs/Geographic Location Study - United States - Wisconsin/Industry - Machinery

183. Lynch, Mary Kathryn. "Restrictions on Management's Right to Dismiss Workers by Means of Plant Closings or by Workforce Reductions, the Relations between Employers and Public Authorities, and the Role of Collective Bargaining in the United States." <u>Georgia Journal of International and Comparative Law</u>, 16: 2 (Spring 1986): 227-233.

    Collective Bargaining/Legislation - United States

184. Lynd, Staughton. "The Genesis of the Idea of a Community Right to Industrial Property in Youngstown and Pittsburgh, 1977-1987." Journal of American History, 74: 3 (Dec. 1987): 926-958.

     Employee Ownership/Impact - Community - Case Studies/ Geographic Location Study - United States - Ohio/Right of Property

185. Maida, Carl A.; Gordon, Norma S.; Farberow, Norman L. The Crisis of Competence: Transitional Stress and the Displaced Worker. (Brunner/Mazel psychosocial stress series ; no. 16) New York: Brunner/Mazel, 1989. 205 p.

     Assistance Programs/Impact - Community/Impact - Psychological - Case Studies

186. Mann, Eric. "Keeping GM Van Nuys Open." Labor Research Review, 5: 2 (Fall 1986): 34-44.

     Geographic Location Study - United States - California/ Industry - Automobile/Labor Unions/Preventive Measures

187. Mann, Eric. "New Directions for the U.A.W.: 'Cooperation' or 'Democracy?'." The Nation, 246: 23 (June 11, 1988): 816-818.

     Collective Bargaining/Industry - Automobile/Labor Unions

188. Marx, Gary S.; Robertson, Ann E. "Understanding the New Plant Closing Bill." Bobbin, (Dec. 1988): 30,32.

     Legislation - United States/Worker Adjustment and Retraining Notification Act

189. Massey, Bill. "Employer Notice of Plant Closings Becomes Law." Arkansas Lawyer, 22: 4 (Oct. 1988): 205-207.

     Legislation - United States/Worker Adjustment and Retraining Notification Act

190. Matlack, Carol. "Forewarning." <u>National Journal</u>, 20 (June 11, 1988): 1534-1537.

Advance Notice/Legislation - Canada/Legislation - United States

191. Matte, Harry. "Cheese Plant Closing Opens New Doors." <u>Personnel Administrator</u>, (Jan. 1988): 52-56.

Assistance Programs/Economic Development Programs/Geographic Location Study - United States - Ohio/Industry - Food Processing - Case Studies/Public Relations

192. Maunders, Allen. <u>A Process of Struggle: The Campaign for Corby Steelmaking in 1979</u>. Aldershot, Hampshire, England: Gower Pub. Co., 1987. 283 p.

Industry - Steel - Case Studies/Geographic Location Study - Great Britain/Labor Unions

193. Maxwell, Nan L. "Labor Market Effects from Involuntary Job Losses in Layoffs, Plant Closings: The Role of Human Capital in Facilitating Reemployment and Reduced Wage Losses." <u>American Journal of Economics and Sociology</u>, 48: 2 (Apr. 1989): 129-141.

Economic Models/Impact - Earnings/Reemployment/Retraining

194. McDermott, Michael C. <u>Multinationals: Foreign Divestment and Disclosure</u>. New York: McGraw-Hill, 1989. 127 p.

Geographic Location Study - Great Britain/Multinational Corporations

195. McGuire, J. P. "Management's Right to Relocate Its Plant and to Make Similar Decisions: Recent Developments." <u>Labor Law Journal</u>, 38: 12 (Dec. 1987): 747-55.

Collective Bargaining - Duty to Bargain/Court or Board Decisions/Labor-Management Relations

196. McHugh, Rick. "Basics of the Plant Closing Notification Law."
     Clearinghouse Review, 23: 8 (Jan. 1989): 932-936.

     Legislation - United States/Worker Adjustment and Retraining
     Notification Act

197. McKenzie, Richard B. "How Big Is the Displaced Worker
     Problem?" Society, 26: 3 (Mar./Apr. 1989): 43-48.

     Data Analysis/Government Programs/Impact - Economic/
     Unemployed

198. McKenzie, Richard B.; Ford, William D. "Advance Plant Closing
     Bill -- Bomb or Balm? The 'Metzen Bomb': Costly Penalties
     for Closing Plants/Advance Notice of Plant Closings: Make It
     the Law." Management Review, (Oct. 1987): 53-54.

     Advance Notice/Impact - Economic/Legislation - United States

199. McLaughlin, Mark. "Closing of GM Plant May Be 'Indefinite,'
     but Prospects down the Road Are Grim." New England Business,
     (Dec. 7, 1987): 52-53.

     Geographic Location Study - United States - Massachusetts/
     Industry - Automobile - Case Studies

200. McLaughlin, Mark. "Colonial Fate Unclear as Boston Rejects Use
     of Eminent Domain." New England Business, (Apr. 7, 1986):
     40-41.

     Geographic Location Study - United States - Massachusetts/
     Impact - Community/Industry - Food Processing/Right of
     Property

201. McTiernan, M. P. Workers' Alternative Plans: A Case Study at
     United Biscuits' Liverpool Plant. (Warwick papers in
     industrial relations ; no. 7) Coventry: Industrial
     Relations Research Unit, School of Industrial and Business
     Studies, University of Warwick, 1986. 13 leaves.

     Geographic Location Study - Great Britain/Labor Unions/
     Preventive Measures - Case Studies

202. Merwin, John. "Mahwah." _Forbes_,   (May 5, 1986): 68-72.

Geographic Location Study - United States - New Jersey/
Impact - Economic/Industry - Automobile/Reemployment

203. Micallef, Charles N.; Cochrane, Brenda; Mangum, Stephen L.
"Role of Labor Educators in Addressing the Needs of
Displaced Workers." _Labor Studies Journal_, 13: 2 (Summer
1988): 28-40.

Geographic Location Study - United States - Ohio/Impact -
Community/Industry - Electrical - Case Studies/Labor Unions/
Retraining

204. Miles, John L. "Legal Notice: Plant Closing Law Covers
Healthcare Facilities, Too." _Health Progress_, 70: 2 (Mar.
1989): 54-56.

Industry - Health Care/Legislation - United States/Worker
Adjustment and Retraining Notification Act

205. _Military Base Closures: Federal Programs to Assist Civilian
Employees and Their Communities_. Washington, D.C.: Public
Employee Department, AFL-CIO, 1989. 21 p.

Assistance Programs/Government Programs/Industry - Defense

206. Millspaugh, Peter E. "Comprehensive Plant Closing Legislation:
Remodeling for Success." _Seton Hall Legislative Journal_, 11:
2 (Winter 1988): 267-293.

Legislation - United States/Legislation - United States -
States

207. Millspaugh, Peter E. "The Managerial Prerogative in Business
Closings: A Legal and Policy Perspective." _University of
Toledo Law Review_, 19: 1 (Fall 1987): 1-40.

Collective Bargaining/Collective Bargaining - Duty to
Bargain/Legislation - United States

208. Millspaugh, Peter E. "Plant Closing Ethics Root in American Law." Journal of Business Ethics, 9: 8 (Aug. 1990): 665-670.

Court or Board Decisions/Ethics/Legislation - United States

209. Mishel, Lawrence R. Advance Notice of Plant Closings: Benefits Outweigh the Costs. (Briefing paper) Washington, D.C.: Economic Policy Institute, 1988. 13 p.

Advance Notice/Impact - Earnings/Unemployed

210. Mishel, Lawrence R. "Advance Notice of Plant Closings: Benefits Outweigh the Costs." Challenge, (July/Aug. 1988): 58-61.

Advance Notice/Impact - Earnings/Reemployment

211. Mishel, Lawrence R.; George, Calvin H. Dislocation and Adjustment: The Impact on Women and Minority Workers. (NCFE special analysis) Washington, D.C.: National Committee for Full Employment, 1987. 10 leaves.

Impact - Minorities/Impact - Women/Unemployed

212. Mishel, Lawrence R.; Podgursky, Michael. "The Incidence of Displacement." Industrial Relations Research Association. Proceedings of the Fortieth Annual Meeting, (Dec. 28-30, 1987): 118-124.

Unemployed

213. Miskovic, Darlene. A Study of Attitudes Associated with Retraining: Part I. Washington, D.C.: National Association of Broadcasters, 1986. 26 p.

Impact - Employees/Retraining - Case Studies

214. Miskovic, Darlene. <u>A Study of Attitudes Associated with</u>
     <u>Retraining: Part II</u>. Washington, D.C.: National Association
     of Broadcasters, 1987. 20 p.

     Retraining

215. Montero, Cecilia Casassus. "Aspetti corporativi della
     modernizzazione nella Francia socialista." <u>Sociologia del</u>
     <u>Lavoro</u>, 26-27 (1986): 349-365.

     Geographic Location Study - France/Labor-Management
     Relations/Legislation - France

216. Moore, Thomas S. "The Nature and Unequal Incidence of Job
     Displacement Costs." <u>Social Problems</u>, 37: 2 (May 1990):
     230-242.

     Data Analysis/Impact - Earnings/Impact - Minorities/Impact -
     Women/Unemployed

217. Moskal, Brian S. "Auto Talks Require Enlightenment." <u>Industry</u>
     <u>Week</u>, 239: 13 (July 2, 1990)

     Collective Bargaining/Employment Security/Industry -
     Automobile/Labor Unions

218. Mullin, John R.; Armstrong, Jeanne H.; Kavanagh, Jean S. "From
     Mill Town to Mill Town: The Transition of a New England Mill
     Town from a Textile to a High-Technology Economy." <u>Journal</u>
     <u>of the American Planning Association</u>, (Winter 1986): 47-59.

     Geographic Location Study - United States - Massachusetts/
     Impact - Community - Case Studies/Industry - Textile/
     Planning Programs

219. Munger, Peter F.; Munger, Stephen X.; Munger, Thomas J. "Plant
     Closures and Relocations under the National Labor Relations
     Act." <u>Georgia State University Law Review</u>, 5: 1 (Fall 1988):
     77-116.

     Collective Bargaining - Duty to Bargain/Discrimination/
     National Labor Relations Act/Plant Relocation

220. Myers, Howard N. "The Ever Changing Labor-management Environment." Labor Law Journal, 37: 4 (Apr. 1986): 250-255.

    Collective Bargaining - Duty to Bargain/Court or Board Decisions/Labor-Management Relations

221. National Foundation for the Study of Employment Policy. Corporate Compliance with the Plant Closing Law: Legal Overview and Selected Legislative History. Washington, D.C.: The Foundation, 1989.

    Legislation - United States/Worker Adjustment and Retraining Notification Act

222. Nelson-Horchler, Joani. "A Specter of Textiles' Future: More Towns May Share Ware Shoals' Fate." Industry Week, 229 (May 26, 1986): 103-106.

    Foreign Competition/Geographic Location Study - United States - South Carolina/Impact - Community/Industry - Textile - Case Studies

223. Nelson-Horchler, Joani. "Two Months' Plant-closing Notice?" Industry Week, 234 (July 27, 1987): 15-16.

    Advance Notice/Legislation - United States

224. Newman, David G.; Gardner, William. Business Closings and Worker Readjustment: The Canadian Approach. Washington, D.C,: National Center on Occupational Readjustment, 1987. 49 leaves.

    Geographic Location Study - Canada/Government Programs/ Legislation - Canada

225. Newman, Lewis. "Hospital Closure: Managing the Pain of Going Out of Business." Healthcare Forum, (July/Aug. 1987): 35-37.

    Assistance Programs/Geographic Location Study - United States - California/Human Resource Planning/Industry - Hospitals - Case Studies

226. Nissen, Bruce. "Union Battles Against Plant Closings: Case Study Evidence and Policy Implications." <u>Policy Studies Journal</u>, 18: 2 (Winter 1990): 382-395.

    Geographic Location Study - United States - Indiana/Impact - Community/Labor Unions

227. <u>Notice Requirements for Plant Closings and Mass Layoffs: Worker Adjustment and Retraining Notification Act: Law and Explanation</u>. Chicago, Ill.: Commerce Clearing House, 1988. 23 p.

    Legislation - United States/Worker Adjustment and Retraining Notification Act

228. O'Brien, Francis T. "Creative Alternatives to Plant Closings: The Rationale for Notice." <u>Labor Law Journal</u>, 38: 8 (Aug. 1987): 458-460.

    Advance Notice/Legislation - United States

229. O'Brien, Maurice W. "Plant Closure and Relocation and the Duty to Bargain." <u>Bench & Bar of Minnesota</u>, (July 1986): 24-31.

    Collective Bargaining - Duty to Bargain/Court or Board Decisions

230. O'Farrell, P. N.; Crouchley, R. "Manufacturing-Plant Closures: A Dynamic Survival Model." <u>Environment and Planning A</u>, 19 (1987): 313-329.

    Causes/Data Analysis/Economic Models/Geographic Location Study - Ireland

231. <u>Ohio's Training Resources for Workers Displaced by Plant Closings</u>. Westerville, Ohio: Council on Vocational Education, 1988. 25 p.

    Assistance Programs/Geographic Location Study - United States - Ohio/Impact - Community - Case Studies/Retraining

232. Ontario. Legislative Assembly. Standing Committee on Resources Development. <u>Report on Plant Closures and Community and Employee Adjustment: 3rd Session, 33rd Parliament, 36 Elizabeth II</u>. Toronto, Ont.: Standing Committee on Resources Development, 1987. 76 p.

Assistance Programs/Geographic Location Study - Canada - Ontario

233. Oulton, Nicholas. "Plant Closures and the Productivity 'Miracle' in Manufacturing." <u>National Institute Economic Review</u>, (Aug. 1987): 53-59.

Geographic Location Study - Great Britain/Productvity

234. Pappas, Gregory. <u>The Magic City: Unemployment in a Working-Class Community</u>. (Anthropology of contemporary issues) Ithaca, N.Y.: Cornell University Press, 1989. 204 p.

Geographic Location Study - United States - Ohio/Impact - Economic/Impact - Psychological/Industry - Rubber - Case Studies/Unemployed

235. Pascarella, Perry. "When Change Means Saying: 'You're Fired'." <u>Industry Week</u>, 230 (July 7, 1986): 47+.

Assistance Programs/Corporate Planning

236. Perkins, Donald S. "What Can CEOs Do for Displaced Workers?" <u>Harvard Business Review</u>, (Nov./Dec. 1987): 90-93.

Assistance Programs/Corporate Planning/Industry - Brewing - Case Studies

237. <u>Permanent Mass Layoffs and Plant Closings, 1987</u>. (Bulletin ; 2310) Washington, D.C.: Bureau of Labor Statistics, 1988. 92 p.

Layoff/Statistical Sources

238. Petchers, Marcia K.; Swanker, Sandra; Singer, Mark I. "The Hospital Merger: Its Effect on Employees." <u>Health Care Management Review</u>, 13: 4 (Fall 1988): 9-14.

    Acquisitions and Mergers/Impact - Employees - Case Studies/ Impact - Psychological/Industry - Hospitals

239. Pichierri, Angelo. "Diagnosi e strategia nel declino della siderurgia europea." <u>Quaderni di Sociologia</u>, 33: 8 (1987): 18-48.

    Economic Development Programs/Geographic Location Study - Europe/Industry - Steel

240. Picot, Gerhard. "Closure of Plants and Other Operational Companies in West Germany." <u>International Business Lawyer</u>, (Feb. 1988): 59-62.

    Geographic Location Study - West Germany/Legislation - West Germany

241. Pipkorn, J. "Voluntary Plant Closings and Workforce Reductions in the European Communities." <u>Georgia Journal of International and Comparative Law</u>, 16: (Spring 1986): 259-265.

    Cooperation/Geographic Location Study - Europe/Legislation - Europe

242. Pitta, Julie. "Pain at National." <u>Forbes</u>, 146: 10 (Oct. 29, 1990): 138.

    Foreign Competition/Industry - Electronics

243. <u>Plant Closing: Advance Notice and Rapid Response: Special Report</u>. Washington, D.C.: Congress of the U.S., Office of Technology Assessment, 1986. 60 p.

    Advance Notice/Assistance Programs/Government Programs

244. Plant Closings: Information on Advance Notice and Assistance
     to Dislocated Workers: Briefing Report to the Chairman,
     Subcommittee on Labor, Committee on Labor and Human
     Resources, United States Senate. Washington, D.C., United
     States General Accounting Office. 1987. 11 p.

     Advance Notice/Assistance Programs

245. Plant Closings: International Context and Social Costs.
     (Social institutions and social change) New York: A. de
     Gruyter, 1988. 193 p. By Carolyn Perrucci et al.

     Impact - Family/Impact - Psychological/International
     Comparative Study

246. Plant Closings: The Complete Resource Guide. (BNA special
     report) Washington, D.C.: Bureau of National Affairs, 1988.
     312 p.

     Case Studies/Legislation - United States - States/Worker
     Adjustment and·Retraining Notification Act

247. A Plant Closure Study: An Administrative Records Search of
     Five Plant Closures in Montana. Helena, MT: Research &
     Analysis Bureau, Dept. of Labor & Industry, 1986. 40 p.

     Case Studies/Geographic Location Study - United States -
     Montana

248. Podgursky, Michael; Swaim, Paul. "Job Displacement and
     Earnings Loss: Evidence from the Displaced Worker Survey/Job
     Loss and Job Change: Comment." Industrial and Labor
     Relations Review, 41: 1 (Oct. 1987): 17-29,45-46,49.

     Data Analysis/Impact - Earnings

249. Politics of Industrial Closure. Houndmills, Basingstoke,
     Hampshire: Macmillan Press, 1987. 201 p. Edited by Tony
     Dickson and David Judge.

     Deindustrialization/Geographic Location Study - Great
     Britain/Impact - Community/Preventive Measures

250. Popham, Mitchell J. "Plant Closure Legislation in the United States: Insights from Great Britain." <u>Loyola of Los Angeles International and Comparative Law Journal</u>, 8 (Spring 1986): 277-299.

   International Comparative Study/Legislation - Great Britain/ Legislation - United States

251. Portz, John. <u>The Politics of Plant Closings</u>. (Studies in government and public policy) Lawrence, Kan.: University Press of Kansas, 1990. 214 p.

   Case Studies/Geographic Location Study - United States - Iowa/Geographic Location Study - United States - Kemtucky/ Geographic Location Study - United States - Pennsylvania/ Political Aspects

252. <u>Protracted Struggle and the Working Class</u>. London: Communist Party of Britain (Marxist-Leninist), 1986. 20 p.

   Geographic Location Study - Great Britain/Industry - Mining/ Labor Unions

253. Ranney, David C. "Combatting Plant Closings: The Role of Labor." <u>Quarterly Journal of Ideology</u>, 10: 4 (Oct. 1986): 61-68.

   Causes - Technological Change/Industry - Mining/Labor Unions/Preventive Measures

254. Ranney, David C. "Manufacturing Job Loss and Early Warning Indicators." <u>Journal of Planning Literature</u>, 3: 1 (Winter 1988): 22-35.

   Case Studies/Causes/Geographic Location Study - United States - Illinois

255. Rasnic, Carol D. "Polygraphs and Plant Closings." <u>Case & Comment</u>, (Jan.-Feb. 1989): 15-21.

   Legislation - United States/Worker Adjustment and Retraining Notification Act

256. Redundancy, Layoffs, and Plant Closures: Their Character, Causes and Consequences. London: Croom Helm, 1987. 339 p. Edited by Raymond M. Lee.

   Causes/Impact/Layoff/Unemployed

257. Report on Mass Layoffs and Plant Closings in 1986. Washington, D.C.: Bureau of Labor Statistics, 1987.

   Layoff/Statistical Sources

258. Responding to Economic Dislocation: Assistance Programs for Unemployed Steelworkers and a Directory of District Programs. Pittsburgh: United Steelworkers of America, 1986. 88 p. Prepared by the International Headquarters Task Force for Dislocated Worker Program Development; presented to the 23rd Constitutional Convention of the United Steelworkers of America.

   Assistance Programs/Directories/Industry - Steel/Retraining

259. Reynolds, Larry. "What Is Adequate Notice of a Plant Closing?" Management Review, (May 1987): 16,18.

   Advance Notice

260. Reynolds, Stanley S. "Plant Closings and Exit Behaviour in Declining Industries." Economica, 55: 220 (Nov. 1988): 493-503.

   Causes - Economic/Economic Models

261. Rhine, Barbara. "Business Closings and Their Effects on Employees -- Adaptation of the Tort of Wrongful Discharge." Industrial Relations Law Journal, 8: 3 (1986): 362-400.

   Court or Board Decisions/Employment at Will/Impact - Employees

262. Rische-Braun, Doris. <u>Betriebliche und gewerkschaftliche</u>
<u>Interessenvertretung bei Personalabbau am Beispiel der</u>
<u>chemiefasererzeugenden Industrie</u>. Frankfurt: R.G. Fischer,
1986. 195 p.

Geographic Location Study - West Germany/Industry - Textile

263. Roberts, Scott Dennis. <u>Resource Allocation and Other Effects</u>
<u>of Structural Unemployment: A Naturalistic Approach</u>. Ph.D.
Dissertation, University of Utah, 1988. 198 leaves.

Impact - Earnings/Impact - Employees/Industry - Steel/
Unemployed

264. Robinson, James C. "Job Hazards and Job Security." <u>Journal of</u>
<u>Health Politics, Policy and Law</u>, 11: 1 (Spring 1986): 1-18.

Layoff/Occupational Safety

265. Romero, Gloria J.; Castro, Felipe G.; Cervantes, Richard C.
"Latinas without Work: Family, Occupational, and Economic
Stress Following Unemployment." <u>Psychology of Women</u>
<u>Quarterly</u>, 12 (Sept. 1988): 281-297.

Data Analysis/Impact - Family/Impact - Psychological/Impact
- Women

266. Rommelspacher, Thomas. "Krupp-Rheinhausen: A Conflict over
the Consequences of Decline in the West German Steel
Industry." <u>International Journal of Urban and Regional</u>
<u>Research</u>, 12: 4 (Dec. 1988): 627-635.

Geographic Location Study - West Germany/Impact - Community/
Industry - Steel/Labor Unions

267. Romo, Frank P.; Korman, Hyman; Brantley, Peter; Schwartz,
Michael. "The Rise and Fall of Regional Political Economies:
A Theory of the Core." <u>Research in Politics and Society</u>, 3
(1988): 37-64.

Causes - Economic/Deindustrialization/Impact - Community/
Foreign Competition/Plant Relocation

268. Root, Kenneth. "Job Loss: Whose Fault, What Remedies?"
     <u>Research in Politics and Society</u>, 3 (1988): 65-84.

     Impact - Social/Preventive Measures/Unemployed

269. Ropp, Kirkland. "Downsizing Strategies: Reducing the Trauma
     of Reducing Employees." <u>Personnel Administrator</u>, 32: 2 (Feb.
     1987): 61-64.

     Corporate Planning/Layoff

270. Ropp, Kirkland. "Restructuring: Survival of the Fittest."
     <u>Personnel Administrator</u>, 32: 2 (Feb. 1987): 45-47.

     Corporate Planning/Human Resource Planning

271. Rosen, Ellen Israel. <u>Bitter Choices: Blue-Collar Women in and
     out of Work</u>. Chicago: University of Chicago Press, 1987. 220
     p.

     Geographic Location Study - United States - New England/
     Impact - Family/Impact - Women/Women in Labor Unions

272. Rothstein, Lawrence E. <u>Plant Closings: Power, Politics, and
     Workers</u>. Dover, Mass.: Auburn House, 1986. 201 p.

     Geographic Location Study - France/International Comparative
     Study/Legislation - France/Legislation - United States

273. Russell, J. Bradley. "Implied Contracts and Creating a
     Corporate Tort: One Way State and Local Government Are
     Starting to Fight Plant Closings." <u>West Virginia Law Review</u>,
     90 (Summer 1988): 1249-1278.

     Court or Board Decisions/Impact - Community/Legislation -
     United States - States

274. Rydzel, James A. "Plant-Closing Legislation -- Living with Prenotification." <u>Employment Relations Today</u>, 15: 4 (Winter 1988/89): 271-277.

Advance Notice/Corporate Planning/Worker Adjustment and Retraining Notification Act

275. Salzman, Jeffrey D. "Canadian-American Plant Closing Demonstration Project." <u>Compensation & Benefits Management</u>, 3: 4 (Summer 1987): 233-239.

Assistance Programs/Geographic Location Study - Canada/ Labor-Management Relations

276. Samborn, Randall. "A Fizzling 'Time Bomb'." <u>National Law Journal</u>, 12: 20 (Jan. 22, 1990): 1, 30-31.

Court or Board Decisions/Worker Adjustment and Retraining Notification Act

277. Schippani, Michael. "Creative Alternatives to Plant Closings: The Massachusetts Experience." <u>Labor Law Journal</u>, 38: 8 (Aug. 1987): 460-464.

Assistance Programs/Geographic Location Study - United States - Massachusetts/Legislation - United States - Massachusetts/Preventive Measures - Case Studies

278. Schippani, Michael. "Massachusetts & Mature Industries." <u>Labor Research Review</u>, 5: 2 (Fall 1986): 79-87.

Economic Development Programs/Geographic Location Study - United States - Massachusetts/Government Programs/Labor Unions/Legislation - United States - Massachusetts

279. Schweke, William; Jones, David R. "European Job Creation in the Wake of Plant Closings and Layoffs." <u>Monthly Labor Review</u>, (Oct. 1986): 18-22.

Geographic Location Study - Europe/Government Programs/ International Comparative Study/Job Creation

280. Sculnick, Michael W. "Plant Closings and Mass Layoffs --
     Toward a Cooperative Approach." _Employment Relations Today_,
     14 (Summer 1987): 99-106.

     Advance Notice/Assistance Programs/Government Programs/
     Labor-Management Relations

281. Seitchik, Adam. _Labor Displacement within the New Family_
     Economy. Ph.D. Dissertation, Boston University, 1988. 190
     leaves.

     Impact - Earnings/Impact - Family/Impact - Women

282. Seitchik, Adam; Zornitsky, Jeffrey. _From One Job to the Next:_
     Worker Adjustment in a Changing Labor Market. Kalamazoo:
     W.E. Upjohn Institute for Employment Research, 129 p.

     Data Analysis/Government Programs/Reemployment/Retraining

283. Sethi, S. Prakash. "The Ax Man Cometh: GM Pulls Out of Norwood
     City." _Business and Society Review_, (Spring 1989): 20-25.

     Cooperation/Geographic Location Study - United States -
     Ohio/Impact - Community/Industry - Automobile - Case Studies

284. Shandor, B. Donald. "The Plant-Closing Law: New Pressures on
     Acquirers." _Mergers & Acquisitions_, (July/Aug. 1989):
     65-68.

     Acquisitions and Mergers/Legislation - United States/Worker
     Adjustment and Retraining Notification Act

285. Shapira, Philip. _Industrial Restructuring and Worker_
     Transition in California Manufacturing. (Working paper ;
     no. 452) Berkeley: Institute of Urban and Regional
     Development, University of California, 1987. 70 p.

     Data Analysis/Geographic Location Study - United States -
     California/Industry - Manufacturing/Job Creation/Unemployed

286. Shapira, Philip. <u>Industry and Jobs in Transition: A Study of Industrial Restructuring and Worker Displacement in California</u>. Ph.D Dissertation, University of California, Berkeley, 1986. 457 leaves.

   Causes/Geographic Location Study - United States - California/Impact - Employees

287. Sheets, Kenneth R.; Seamonds, Jack A. "Nomadic Quests for a Decent Break." <u>U.S. News & World Report</u>, 101 (Sept. 29, 1986): 51-52.

   Employee Relocation - Case Studies/Unemployed

288. Sheridan, John H. "Easing the Sting: Wapakoneta Shutdown Sets an Example." <u>Industry Week</u>, 233 (June 29, 1987): 16-17.

   Geographic Location Study - United States - Ohio/Industry - Food Processing/Reemployment Planning - Case Studies

289. Shultz, David; Jann, David. "The Use of Eminent Domain and Contractually Implied Property Rights to Affect Business and Plant Closings." <u>William Mitchell Law Review</u>, 16: 2 (Spring 1990): 383-427.

   Court or Board Decisions/Impact - Community/Right of Property - Case Studies

290. Siegel, Jay S. "Lack of Knowledge Is a Dangerous Thing." <u>New England Business</u>, (Mar. 7, 1988): 73-74.

   Geographic Location Study - United States - Connecticut/ Legislation - United States - Connecticut

291. Siegel, Lewis B. "BLS Surveys Mass Layoffs and Plant Closings in 1986." <u>Monthly Labor Review</u>, (Oct. 1987): 39-40.

   Data Analysis/Layoff

292. Singer, Joseph William. "The Reliance Interest in Property." _Stanford Law Review_, 40: 3 (Feb. 1988): 611-751.

     Industry - Steel/Legislation - United States/Right of Property

293. Smith, Suzanna D. _Women and Plant Closings: Job Loss and Subsequent Labor Force Activities_. Ph.D. Dissertation, University of Georgia, 1988. 163 leaves.

     Impact - Women/Reemployment/Retraining

294. Smith, Suzanna D.; Price, Sharon J. _Women and Plant Closings: Unemployment, Reemployment, and Job Training Enrollment Following Dislocation_. Philadelphia: National Council on Family Relations, 1988. 34 p. Paper presented at the Annual Meeting of the National Council on Family Relations (50th, Philadelphia, PA, November 12-16, 1988).

     Impact - Women/Reemployment/Retraining/Unemployed

295. Solovy, Alden T. "Plant Closing Provision Would Include Hospitals." _Hospitals_, 62: 12 (June 20, 1988): 28.

     Industry - Hospitals/Legislation - United States

296. Squire, Catherine Alison. _Transforming People and an Organization: Transition to Employee Ownership and Democratic Management at the Rath Packing Company, 1979-1982_. Master's Thesis, Cornell University, 1989. 230 p.

     Employee Ownership - Case Studies/Geographic Location Study - United States - Iowa/Industry - Meat Packing/Labor Unions

297. Stack, Bill. "Survival Tactics: When the Facility Must Close Down." _Management Review_, 79: 5 (May 1990): 54-57.

     Assistance Programs/Corporate Planning - Case Studies/ Industry - Telecommunications/Labor-Management Relations

298. Starling, Grover; Baskin, Otis W. "A Systems Approach to Plant Closings." <u>Akron Business and Economic Review</u>, 17: 4 (Winter 1986): 108-121.

    Corporate Planning/Impact - Community/Impact - Economic

299. Staudohar, Paul D. "New Plant Closing Law Aids Workers in Transition." <u>Personnel Journal</u>, 68: 1 (Jan. 1989): 87-90.

    Advance Notice/Worker Adjustment and Retraining Notification Act

300. Steinberg, Danny; Monforte, Frank A. <u>Estimating the Effects of Job Search Assistance and Training Programs on the Unemployment Durations of Displaced Workers</u>. (Discussion paper ; 86-15) San Diego, Calif.: Department of Economics, University of California, San Diego, 1986. 29 p.

    Assistance Programs/Data Analysis/Retraining/Unemployed

301. Stepanek, Marcia. "Reader's Digest Employees Refuse to Go Home: The Long Goodbye." <u>Far Eastern Economic Review</u>, (Mar. 8, 1990): 32-33.

    Geographic Location Study - Japan/Industry - Publishing/ Labor Unions

302. "Still Time for a New Strategy." <u>Economist</u>, (May 26, 1990): 63-64.

    Geographic Location Study - Scotland/Industry - Steel

303. Stoffman, Daniel. "Where Everyone Fears to Tread." <u>Canadian Business</u>, 61: 6 (June 1988): 54-58, 243-247.

    Foreign Competition/Geographic Location Study - Canada/ Industry - Tires/Multinational Corporations

304. Storlie, Rebecca; Park, Rosemarie. *A Preliminary AVTI/Agency Cooperative Model for Serving the Needs of Dislocated Workers in Minnesota*. St. Paul: Minnesota State Board of Vocational-Technical Education, 1986. 34 p.

   Assistance Programs/Geographic Location Study - United States - Minnesota/Government Programs/Retraining

305. Sudbury, Deborah A. "The Final Rule Under WARN: Beset with Pitfalls for the Unwary." *Employee Relations Law Journal*, 15: 1 (Summer 1989): 147-156.

   Corporate Planning/Legislation - United States/Worker Adjustment and Retraining Notification Act

306. Susser, Peter A. "Election-Year Politics and the Enactment of Federal 'Plant-Closing' Legislation." *Employee Relations Law Journal*, (Winter 1988/89): 349-358.

   Advance Notice/Legislation - United States/Worker Adjustment and Retraining Notification Act

307. Sutton, Robert I. "The Process of Organizational Death: Disbanding and Reconnecting." *Administrative Science Quarterly*, 32: 4 (Dec. 1987): 542-569.

   Case Studies/Impact/Organizational Behavior

308. Swinney, Dan; Metzgar, Jack. "Expanding the Fight against Shutdowns." *Labor Research Review*, 5: 2 (Fall 1986): 99-112.

   Economic Development Programs/Industry - Manufacturing/Labor Unions/Preventive Measures

309. Taber, Tom D.; Cooke, Robert A.; Walsh, Jeffrey T. "A Joint Business-Community Approach to Improve Problem Solving by Workers Displaced in a Plant Shutdown." *Journal of Community Psychology*, 18: 1 (Jan. 1990): 19-33.

   Assistance Programs - Case Studies/Impact - Community/Impact - Employees

310. Targ, Harry R.; Perrucci, Robert; Perrucci, Carolyn; Targ, Dena. "Worker Responses to Plant Closings." <u>Labor Law Journal</u>, 39: 8 (Aug. 1988): 562-566.

    Data Analysis/Impact - Employees/Unemployed

311. <u>Technology and Structural Unemployment: Reemploying Displaced Adults</u>. Washington, D.C.: Office of Technology Assessment, 1986. 445 p.

    Foreign Trade Policy/Government Programs/Reemployment/ Retraining

312. Thompson, Donald B. "Can't Stay, Can't Leave: Huge 'Exit Costs' Multiply Industry's Woes." <u>Industry Week</u>, 233 (June 15, 1987): 26-27.

    Bankruptcy/Industry - Steel/Employee Benefits

313. "Too Much Milling Around." <u>The Economist</u>, (Sept. 26, 1987): 84-85.

    Geographic Location Study - Europe/Industry - Steel

314. Torrence, William D. "Plant Closing and Advance Notice: Another Look at the Numbers." <u>Labor Law Journal</u>, 37: 8 (Aug. 1986): 461-466.

    Advance Notice/Collective Bargaining - Contract Language/ Data Analysis/Reemployment

315. Trousdell, Elizabeth Grace. <u>American and Swedish Strategies for Dealing with Economic Change and Social Dislocation: The Story of Two Mill Towns</u>. Ph.D. Dissertation, Indiana University, 1988. 404 leaves.

    Geographic Location Study - Sweden/Geographic Location Study - United States - Pennsylvania/Government Programs/Impact - Community/Industry - Steel

316. United States. Congress. House. Committee on Education and Labor. <u>Hearing on the Impact of Deregulation on the American Workers ... Hearing Held in Miami, FL. on July 27, 1987</u>. (Serial No. 100-33) Washington, D.C.: U.S. G.P.O., 1987. 109 p.

Acquisitions and Mergers/Impact - Employees/Labor-Management Relations/Legislation - United States

317. United States. Congress. House. Committee on Education and Labor. Subcommittee on Employment Opportunities. <u>Oversight Hearing on the Job Training Partnership Act (Part 3): Hearing ... Ninety-Ninth Congress, First Session (Montebello, CA, November 8, 1985)</u>. Washington, D.C.: U.S. G.P.O., 1986. 58 p.

Job Training Partnership Act/Retraining/Unemployed

318. United States. Congress. House. Committee on Education and Labor. Subcommittee on Labor-Management Relations. <u>Economic Dislocation and Worker Adjustment Assistance Act, H.R. 1122 ... Hearing Held in Washington, D.C., March 17, 1987</u>. Washington, D.C.: U.S.G.P.O., 1988. 292 p.

Assistance Programs/Legislation - United States/Retraining

319. United States. Congress. Senate. Committee on Labor and Human Resources. Subcommittee on Labor. <u>General Motors Plant Closings: Hearing ... January 26, 1987, Norwood, OH</u>. Washington, D.C.: G.P.O., 1987. 125 p.

Causes/Geographic Location Study - United States - Ohio/ Impact - Community/Industry - Automobile

320. United States. General Accounting Office. <u>Dislocated Workers: Extent of Business Closures, Layoffs, and the Public and Private Response: Briefing Report to the Honorable Lloyd Bentsen, United States Senate</u>. Washington, D.C.: U.S. General Accounting Office, 1986. 37 p.

Assistance Programs/Causes/Government Programs/Unemployed

321. United States. General Accounting Office. <u>Plant Closings:</u> <u>Evaluation of Cost Estimate of Proposed Advance Notice</u> <u>Requirement: Report to Congressional Requesters</u>. Washington, D.C.: U.S. General Accounting Office, 1988. 8 p.

Advance Notice/Unemployed

322. United States. General Accounting Office. <u>Plant Closings:</u> <u>Limited Advance Notice and Assistance Provided Dislocated</u> <u>Workers: Report to Congressional Committees</u>. Washington, D.C.: United States General Accounting Office, 1987. 89 p.

Advance Notice/Assistance Programs/Reemployment

323. Verespej, Michael A. "Plant Closings: For Whom the Notice Tolls." <u>Industry Week</u>, (Dec. 5, 1988): 17,20.

Advance Notice/Corporate Planning/Worker Adjustment and Retraining Notification Act

324. Wachter, Michael L.; Cohen, George M. "The Law and Economics of Collective Bargaining: An Introduction and Application to the Problems of Subcontracting, Partial Closure, and Relocation." <u>University of Pennsylvania Law Review</u>, 136: 5 (May 1988): 1349-1417.

Collective Bargaining/Court or Board Decisions/Plant Relocation/Subcontracting

325. Wagel, William H. "New Beginnings for Displaced Workers: Outplacement at GE." <u>Personnel</u>, (Dec. 1988): 12-18.

Industry - Electrical/Reemployment/Retraining

326. Wallace, Cynthia. "Some Troubled Hospitals Discover Creative Solutions to Avoid Closing." <u>Modern Healthcare</u>, (Mar. 13, 1987): 84-88.

Bankruptcy/Industry - Hospitals/Layoff/Preventive Measures

327. Wallace, Michael; Rothschild, Joyce. "Plant Closings, Capital Flight, and Worker Dislocation: The Long Shadow of Deindustrialization." <u>Research in Politics and Society</u>, 3 (1988): 1-35.

Deindustrialization/Impact - Social/Unemployed

328. Watts, H. D.; Stafford, H. A. "Plant Closure and the Multiplant Firm: Some Conceptual Issues." <u>Progress in Human Geography</u>, 10: 2 (1986): 206-227.

Causes - Economic/Multinational Corporations

329. Weg, Howard J. "Introduction to Federal Regulation of Plant Closings and Mass Layoffs." <u>Commercial Law Journal</u>, 94: 2 (Summer 1989): 123-158.

Corporate Planning/Legislation - United States/Worker Adjustment and Retraining Notification Act

330. Weisman, Dan. "Greenhouse: Why a Good Plan Failed." <u>Labor Research Review</u>, 5: 2 (Fall 1986): 88-89.

Geographic Location Study - United States - Rhode Island/Job Creation/Legislation - United States - Rhode Island

331. Weissman, Michael L. "The Plant Closing Laws: A New Threat for Secured Lenders." <u>Secured Lender</u>, (May/June 1989): 16-21.

Acquisitions and Mergers - Case Studies/Impact - Economic/ Legislation - United States - Maine

332. <u>"Wenn es brennt an der Ruhr--!", Hattingen--ein Stadt kämpft!: Tagebuch des Widerstands gegen Arbeitsplatzvernichtung.</u> Hattingen: Betriebsrat und IG Metall-Vertauenskörper der Thyssen Henrichshütte AG [und] IG Metall Verwaltungsstelle Hattingen, 1988. 111 p.

Geographic Location Study - West Germany/Industry - Steel/ Labor Unions

333. Werber, Marilyn; Schmitt, Bill. "Steel Seeks Ways to Cope with Plant-closings Law." _American Metal Market_, (Aug. 4, 1988): 1,6.

   Industry - Steel/Legislation - United States

334. Withington, John. _Shutdown: The Anatomy of a Shipyard Closure_. London: Bedford Square Press, 1989. 166 p.

   Geographic Location Study - Great Britain/Industry - Shipbuilding - Case Studies/Unemployed

335. Wolf, Jerry. "The Closing of Firestone's Albany Plant: A Case Study." _Labor Law Journal_, 37: 8 (Aug. 1986): 466-469.

   Assistance Programs/Geographic Location Study - United States - Georgia/Industry - Tires - Case Studies

336. Wooden, Mark. _Economic Change and Labour Displacement: Managerial Responses & Public Policy_. (Working paper series ; no. 87) Bedford Park, S. Aust.: National Institute of Labour Studies, 1986. 65 p.

   Assistance Programs/Unemployed

337. Wooden, Mark; Sloan, Judy. _The Effects of Redundancy: the Closure of the Rowntree-Hoadley Factory, Adelaide_. (Working paper series ; no. 91) Bedford Park, S. Aust.: National Institute of Labour Studies, 1987. 52 p.

   Geographic Location Study - Australia/Industry - Confectionery - Case Studies

338. Woodworth, Warner. "Steel Busting in the West." _Social Policy_, 18: 3 (Winter 1988): 53-56.

   Geographic Location Study - United States - Utah/Impact - Community/Industry - Steel - Case Studies

339. Woolfson, Charles; Foster, John. <u>Track Record: The Story of the Caterpillar Occupation</u>. London: Verso, 1988. 296 p.

   Geographic Location Study - Scotland/Industry - Agricultural Equipment/Labor Unions/Multinational Corporations

340. <u>Worker Dislocation: Case Studies of Causes and Cures</u>. Kalamazoo, Mich.: W.E. Upjohn Institute for Employment Research, 1987. 219 p. Robert F. Cook, editor.

   Government Programs - Case Studies/Job Training Partnership Act

341. <u>Workplace Education</u>. Boston: Massachusetts State Executive Office of Economic Affairs, 1987. 8 p.

   Geographic Location Study - United States - Massachusetts/ Government Programs/Labor Unions/Skills

342. Wright, Cameron. <u>A Worker's Guide to Plant Closures</u>. Waterloo, Ontario: Waterloo Public Interest Research Group, 1986. 12 p.

   Case Studies/Employee Ownership/Geographic Location Study - Canada - Ontario/Legislation - Canada/Legislation - United States

343. Wright, Robert. "Firing Lines: Free Trade and Plant Closing Notice Law in Congress." <u>The New Republic</u>, 198: 18 (May 2, 1988): 18-20.

   Advance Notice/Foreign Trade Policy/Legislation - United States

344. Wu, Sen-Yuan. <u>Manufacturing Decline and Fiscal Strain of Local Governments in New York State, 1968-1979</u>. Ph.D. Dissertation, State University of New York at Stony Brook, 1987. 162 leaves.

   Causes - Economic/Data Analysis/Deindustrialization/ Geographic Location Study - United States - New York

345. Wu, Sen-Yuan; Korman, Hyman. "Socioeconomic Impacts of Disinvestment on Communities in New York State." <u>American Journal of Economics and Sociology</u>, 47: 3 (July 1987): 261-271.

Geographic Location Study - United States - New York/ Government Programs/Impact - Community/Impact - Economic/ Impact - Social

346. Zeitlin, Morris. "Taking Private Property for Public Use: A Not So Sacred Cow." <u>Political Affairs</u>, 66 (June 1987): 24-28.

Court or Board Decisions/Right of Property

347. Zipp, John F.; Lane, Katherine E. "Plant Closings and Control over the Workplace: A Case Study." <u>Work and Occupations</u>, 14: 1 (Feb. 1987): 62-87.

Corporate Power/Industry - Automobile/Plant Relocation

SUBJECT INDEX

AUTHOR INDEX

Abbey, Michael H.   1

Abrams, James L.   2

Addison, John T.   3, 4, 5, 6

Album, Michael J.   8

Armstrong, Jeanne H.   218

Ashton, Patrick, J.   9

Austin, Phyllis   10

Badenfuller, Charles   12

Bahl, Roy   13

Baker, Andrew M.   14

Balfe, Kevin P.   88, 89

Barbee, George E. L.   15, 16

Barber, Floyd   17

Bartholomew, Susan   18

Baskin, Otis W.   298

Beaird, J. Ralph   19

Beckett, Joyce O.   20

Bee, Richard H.   21

Benenson, Bob   22

Bensman, David   23

Bentley, Marion T.   141

Berenbeim, Ronald   24

Beronja, Terry Ann   21

Berry, Steve   25

Birch, David L.   26

Blanpain, R.   27

Blanquet, F.   28

Bracker, Jeffrey   158

Braddock, David   126

Bradley, Keith   29

Brantley, Peter   267

Brittain, Brian K   30

Broman, Clifford L.   118

Brown, Holly E.   66

Brown, Michelle   64

Browning, Martin   31

Bruno, Robert A   32

Burke, Ronald J.   33

Buss, Terry F.   34

Bussey, Jane   35

Byrne, Edmund F.   36

Cagan, Steve   37

Caplan, Sorrell   38

Carr, Steven D.   39

Carroll, Charles T. Jr.   40

Castro, Felipe G.   41, 265

Cervantes, Richard C.   41, 265

Charpentier, Elaine   42, 176

Christie, Innis   43

Clark, Gordon L.   44

Clavel, Pierre   137

Cochrane, Brenda   47, 48, 203

Gall, Gilbert J.   154

Gallo, Judith   101

Galvin, Martin Jay   102

Gardner, William   224

George, Calvin H.   211

Gerhart, Paul F.   104

Gest, Ted   35

Gibbons, Robert   105

Gibson, W. David   106

Giloth, Robert   107

Gordon, Norma S.   185

Gorney, Carole   108

Gottschalk, Peter   25

Gould, William B., IV   109

Grayson, J. Paul   110, 111

Griffin, Gerard   64

Guskind, Robert   112

Hamermesh, Daniel S.   113, 114, 115, 116, 117

Hamilton, V. Lee   118

Hampton, William J.   119

Hanratty, Patricia   137

Hansen, Gary B.   120, 121, 122, 123, 124

Hardy, Cynthia   125

Harris, Michael M.   126

Harris, Stanley G.   127

Harte, G. F.   128

United States. Congress. House. Committee on Education and
    Labor. Subcommittee on Labor-Management Relations 318

United States. Congress. Senate. Committee on Labor and Human
    Resources. Subcommittee on Labor 319

United States. General Accounting Office 320, 321, 322

United Steelworkers of America 258

Vaughan, Roger J. 34

Verespej, Michael A. 323

Wachter, Michael L. 324

Wagel, William H. 325

Wallace, Cynthia 326

Wallace, Michael 327

Walsh, Jeffrey T. 309

Watts, H. D. 328

Weg, Howard J. 329

Weisman, Dan 330

Weissman, Barbara J. 178

Weissman, Michael L. 331

Werber, Marilyn 334

Whyte, William F. 178

Wissoker, Doug 25

Withington, John 333

Wolf, Jerry 335

Wooden, Mark 336, 337

Woodworth, Warner 338

Woolfson, Charles 339

Wright, Cameron 342